LAND
JOHN O'

C000063705

The Official Cyclist's Challenge Guide

910 Miles Through England,
Wales and Scotland
on
The Shortest Cycling Route by Road

Brian Smailes

Brian Smailes

Holds the record for the fastest 4 and 5 continuous crossings of the Lyke Wake Walk over the North York Moors. He completed the 210 miles over rough terrain on 5 crossings in June 1995 taking 85 hours and 50 minutes. In 2008 he completed his 53rd crossing.
An expedition in 2008 took him to the jungles around Canaima in Venezuela, exploring on foot and by dugout canoe the tributaries of the Rio Carrao up to Angel Falls.

China's Great Wall expedition in 2007 involved walking sections in remote areas along the former borders of Mongolia.

On a 2005 expedition, Brian walked the Inca Trail in Peru, visiting Lake Titticacca and Bolivia while in the area.

In August 2003 he walked from John O'Groats to Lands End, completing it in 34 days. In August 2001 he cycled from Lands End to John O`Groats, a journey of over 910 miles in 6 days 13 hours 18 minutes. This involved carrying food, clothing and tent, and was completed without support between both ends. A further cycle ride, this time from John O'Groats to Lands End took place in July 2007 to complete the two-way cycle crossing.

Having travelled extensively throughout the UK, Europe and the Caribbean, Brian has recently been writing international travel guides to enable the holidaymaker to access the world with ease and enjoy it as much as he does.

Long distance running, canoeing and sub aqua diving are other sports he enjoys, completing 25 marathons and canoeing the Caledonian Canal 3 times.

Brian has dived all around the UK coastline as well as Thailand, Cuba, Venezuela, Egypt and Mexico.

Brian lives in Yorkshire and has walked the hills and dales throughout the County. In compiling this 2nd edition of Lands End to John O'Groats, the route still holds as much pleasure now as it did the first time he cycled it.

Walk Guides

THE YORKSHIRE DALES TOP TEN
ISBN 978-0-9526900-5-4

THE DERBYSHIRE TOP TEN
ISBN 978-1-903568-03-3

THE NATIONAL 3 PEAKS WALK
ISBN 978-1-903568-53-8

ISLE OF WIGHT, NORTH TO SOUTH – EAST TO WEST
ISBN 978-1-903568-07-1

THE SCOTTISH COAST TO COAST WALK
ISBN 978-0-9526900-8-5

THE LYKE WAKE WALK GUIDE
ISBN 978-1-903568-47-7

THE GREAT GLEN WAY
ISBN 978-1-903568-13-2

THE LANCASHIRE TRAIL
ISBN 978-1-903568-10-1

THE 1066 COUNTRY WALK
ISBN 978-1-903568-00-2

THE NOVICES GUIDE TO THE YORKSHIRE 3 PEAKS WALK

ISBN 978 1-903568-46-0

SHORT WALKS IN THE LAKE DISTRICT

ISBN 978-1-903568-20-0

JOHN O'GROATS TO LANDS END (walking)

ISBN 978-1-903568-18-7

WALK HADRIAN'S WALL

ISBN 978-1-903568-40-8

20 WALKS AROUND GLEN NEVIS & FORT WILLIAM

ISBN 978-1-903568-57-6

Cycle Guide

MILLENNIUM CYCLE RIDES IN 1066 COUNTRY

ISBN 978-1-903568-04-0

Obtainable from bookshops or direct from the address or web site below. See web site for book details -

www.chall-pub.co.uk

LANDS END TO JOHN O'GROATS

ISBN 978-1-903568-59-0

Second Edition - 2009

CHALLENGE PUBLICATIONS
7, EARLSMERE DRIVE, BARNSLEY. S71 5HH

CONTENTS

PHOTOGRAPHS

ACKNOWLEDGEMENTS

In publishing this 2nd edition of Lands End to John O'Groats Cycle Guide, I must thank the following people for their help and contribution: -

Pam Smailes and Graham & Sandra Fish for taking me to Lands End.

Graphic Design - Jamie Mann.

First Published   **2004**
Second Edition   **2009**
ISBN 978-1-903568-59-0

Published by Challenge Publications,
7, Earlsmere Drive, Ardsley, Barnsley, S71 5HH.
www.chall-pub.co.uk

The information recorded in this book is believed by the author to be correct at publication. No liabilities can be accepted for any inaccuracies, which may be found. It is recommended that anyone using this book should refer to the relevant map in conjunction with the book and be experienced in map recognition

The description or representation of a route used does not necessarily mean there is existence of a right of way.

INTRODUCTION

The first 'End to End' was recorded in 1879 by Robert Carlyle. Since that time, thousands have completed it in ever increasing numbers. People have attempted this challenge on bicycles, including a penny-farthing bicycle, carried crosses, walked nude, carried doors and bricks, pushed wheelbarrows and travelled by car, wheelchair and aeroplane.

In the early days, cyclists had basic bikes. Penny-farthings were popular and solid tyres were common! The roads were bad and neglected as the popularity of the railways increased. Due to travel on horseback and in coaches, the roads were covered in horse dung, a pleasant sight and smell as our ancestors cycled through the country lanes enjoying their end to end in the 1800's.

The record for cycling end to end was 6 days 16 hours in 1885 set by James Lennox of Dumfries, but by 1965 that was down to under 2 days. The current record is 1 day 20 hours, 4 mins and 19 seconds by cycling! This is of course on a racing bike with full support, riding lightweight non-stop.

One of the more famous people to complete it is Dr. Barbara Moore in the 1960's. She was probably the person who re-awakened people to the challenge when she walked the route. Ian Botham the famous cricketer, his walk was publicised throughout the media and he raised a lot of money for charity.

Lands End to John O'Groats is a minimum of 874 miles but as you cannot cycle on motorways then it will be around the 910-mile mark. Either way it represents a challenge that cannot be taken lightly. To complete this challenge requires dedication, commitment and a sense of purpose. Training the body and mind to cope with the daily distance is an important aspect in your preparation for this ultimate British challenge.

Lands End is the most south-westerly tip of the English mainland, the central point is the signpost (photo 3), which points to John O'Groats, New York and The Isles of Scilly. There is a visitor centre with attractions, shops, café and hotel (photo 4). Lands End itself covers about 100 acres and is an area of natural beauty. Many people visit, especially throughout the summer. The sea around Lands End is a graveyard for ships with many wrecks around it, one of the more famous and recent being the Torey Canyon.

John O'Groats is situated at the northern tip of mainland Scotland with fine views over the Pentland Firth towards the Orkney Islands. Britain's second busiest shipping channel is between these points. There is the last house in Scotland (photo 12), a tourist information centre and a cluster of shops. The famous signpost there points to Lands End, near to the start/finish line, where you end your journey (photo 2). The name John O'Groats dates back to 1496 when three Dutch brothers, the de Groots, worked on the land and sea in that area. Eventually the area became known as John O'Groats.

The journey between both points is long, can be dangerous on the road, and remote in a number of areas, so correct preparation and planning is essential if you are to complete this cycle route. Follow the advice and recommendations in this book then it is down to you and your ability to stay the course for 900 miles.

Between April and October is obviously the best time to attempt this challenge, but the best time would be May/June. This is for a number of reasons: -

The days are long and if you are feeling fit, you can make good progress either early morning or late in the evening.

It is not usually too hot in May/June compared to July/August and you will not be left feeling exhausted because of the heat and having to drink so much to avoid dehydration.

Cycling in May/June means you miss the main holiday time of July/August when B&Bs get booked early and there is a lot more holiday traffic on the roads. Generally it is a lot better to go in May/June.

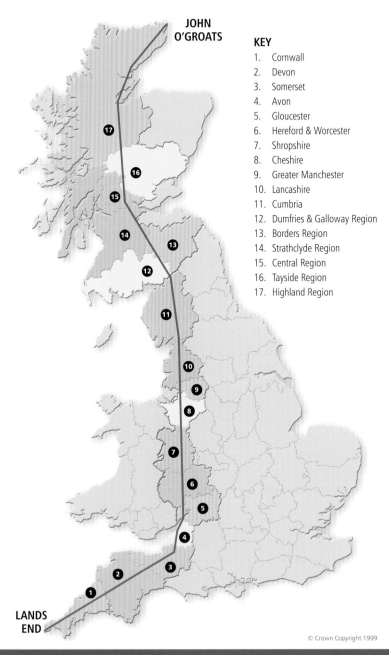

JOHN
O'GROATS

KEY

1. Cornwall
2. Devon
3. Somerset
4. Avon
5. Gloucester
6. Hereford & Worcester
7. Shropshire
8. Cheshire
9. Greater Manchester
10. Lancashire
11. Cumbria
12. Dumfries & Galloway Region
13. Borders Region
14. Strathclyde Region
15. Central Region
16. Tayside Region
17. Highland Region

LANDS
END

© Crown Copyright 1999

THE CHALLENGE

I have described to you in this book what I feel is the shortest route by road baring a few small exceptions. Generally the route is mostly on 'A' roads but ventures onto some minor roads in Devon and Scotland. The route is the main official challenge route used by most cyclists, and if you take another route then you end up cycling further! It usually takes between 6 and 15 days to complete the journey depending if you are a fast or slow cyclist or if you prefer a more leisurely ride, stopping off in most villages on route.

To cycle between 60 and 120 miles a day may seem to some people an easy daily distance, but bear in mind that you do this day in day out and that is the difficult part. Add to this the aching muscles, chafing; numb hands, rain, head on winds and busy traffic, you are in for a hard challenge ahead!

Something that can present a problem is your safety on the road. Wearing something of high visibility is important (photo 5), as is the wearing of a suitable cycling helmet. These and other safety points will be looked at in detail later.

Many people have a support vehicle to accompany them. This is good if you can find someone with the time and vehicle to do it. An estate car where you can sleep in the back is ideal, but any vehicle will do to support you, carry your equipment and supply you with drinks and food on route. On a venture of this type you need to eat regularly, usually little and often to keep your energy levels up.

I found it helpful to take a 'bivi' bag or a lightweight tent, which can be used if there are no B&Bs available as can happen. I have included some B&Bs and the tourist information centres on route. This will help you with your planning

▲ Photo 1. The Start/Finish Line at Lands End

▼ Photo 2. The Start/Finish Line at John O'Groats

Terrain

The remoteness of some areas, particularly in Scotland means that it is wise to carry a small supply of food with you. There are shops in some villages but this often means you need to turn off your route to go into the villages, resulting in cycling extra miles and taking longer for your journey overall. Keep one days rations in your panniers especially when passing through Scotland!

You can generally divide the route into four sections, Lands End to Bristol, Bristol to Carlisle, Carlisle to Inverness and Inverness to John O'Groats. Devon and Cornwall has many hills but usually not too steep, so you can cycle them reasonably well. Somerset was fairly flat, but when you reach The Severn Bridge you have a long drag up to Monmouth from Chepstow.

The central section is not too bad for hills, going through Shrewsbury, Warrington and Preston. This is until you come to Shap Fell after leaving Kendal. Again, it is a long climb up but an exhilarating ride down the other side.

The route is slightly undulating to Carlisle and through the Scottish borders. Cycling on the 'service' road alongside the M74 there are flat sections and long gentle climbs. Arriving in the highlands, the gradients are steeper as you cycle through the Pass of Drumochter up to 459m, and near Inverness and beyond can be steep in parts. Crossing the Black Isle is not too bad, with a run down to the bridge over the Cromarty Firth.

Turning the corner just before Alness, it is fairly easy going to Tain where there is a run down to the bridge crossing the A9. Now it is small undulating hills to cycle over and some flat sections through the villages until you approach Helmsdale to Latherton section. Here there are three very steep hills to ascend and most cyclists get off and walk (photo 10).

You are on the last leg now and the going becomes easier with flat sections and gentle undulations right to the finish at John O'Groats.

I felt that the hardest section was the last one through Scotland. The more exposed area, the head on winds and the hills to climb can make the trip so much harder. Devon and Cornwall presented a lesser problem, although there were many small hills in the area to navigate over. Having to cycle along the A30 in heavy traffic, makes it slightly hazardous, but the dual carriageway is wide and has ample room for cycles on the inside. What kept me going was the thought that what goes up must come down! Remember that and it will get you through.

Now you have an insight into the pleasures and pains on this expedition let us continue our preparation and look at the more detailed planning.

Photo 3. The Famous Signpost at Lands End

PLANNING PHASE

There are a number of aspects to this section so we will look at each part in detail.

The Route

Which is the best direction to do this challenge? Well, most people start from Lands End up to John O'Groats. The reason is that generally the prevailing winds come from the southwest, so you would be travelling with the wind behind you, hopefully. It is not always the case though so be prepared for head on winds at some point on your journey. Other than the prevailing winds, there is no other reason to justify it as far as cycling the route goes.

It is easy planning to cycle a set distance each day, however in practice this can quickly change. You may just be out of energy some days and cannot cycle any further. Weather conditions may be bad some days or there may be cycle problems, e.g. punctures. While taking note where the villages are, cycle as far each day as you feel comfortable with. When I cycled the route, I found it took the first three days to get the muscles used to cycling such a long distance each day, after that, some days I could cycle up to 160 miles a day; on others it was only 100 miles.

Weather

The weather can play a big part in how far you can cycle each day. I found that wearing waterproofs was helpful if I was not sweating, but generally I got wetter wearing them, so later in the journey I resorted to only wearing shorts and t-shirt that are quick drying. The rain may have soaked me but it was refreshing and I cycled a lot quicker and further.

One important point is to ensure that the air temperature is warm enough to enable you to wear the minimum of clothing otherwise you may get hypothermia. Smearing Vaseline on the legs and arms will allow the rain to quickly run off and help to keep you warmer. I can recommend this method providing you have dry clothing in your panniers to use if necessary and you are not cold in the rain.

Which Map?

You need to be familiar with the route well before you leave. There are many detailed maps on the market showing the route described in this book. I suggest getting a map book like the AA large scale road atlas for around £3.99 and cutting out only the relevant sections of the route to take with you. This cuts down on weight and more importantly space. If the sheets are numbered in route order then that saves time.

Highlight the route on the map sections, so you can pick it out at a glance. Doing this will enable you to be prepared for any hills, traffic problems or busy town areas. The individual sheets can be discarded as you finish with them.

Clothing & Equipment

The months before your expedition gives you time to acquire your clothing and equipment. Whatever you buy needs to be strong and durable enough to stand up to the rigours of your expedition. Above all your clothing needs to keep you warm and protected from the elements. Try to purchase light coloured or reflective clothing where possible.

The following list may help you, but each person has different requirements. Remember when packing your cycle bags/panniers that ounces turn into pounds so choose carefully: -

Equipment Checklist

- [ ] 1 Tracksuit
- [ ] Lightweight tent or bivi bag
- [ ] 3 pairs of shorts (high visibility)
- [ ] 3 tops (1 long sleeve, 2 t-shirts) high visibility
- [ ] Water bottles (2 recommended)
- [ ] Small multiple use army knife
- [ ] Mobile phone
- [ ] Elastic bandages/knee supports etc.
- [ ] Sun cream/midge cream/sting relief
- [ ] Travel Wash (for washing clothing)
- [ ] Survival bag/whistle
- [ ] Food/sweets/fruit
- [ ] Cagoul/Overtrousers
- [ ] Sun Glasses
- [ ] Personal items
- [ ] Toilet paper
- [ ] Notepaper/pencil
- [ ] 4 pairs of socks
- [ ] Camera
- [ ] First aid kit
- [ ] Cap/woolly hat
- [ ] Trainers
- [ ] Toiletries, razor etc.
- [ ] Sleeping Bag
- [ ] Gel-gloves
- [ ] Hi-viz waterproof Jacket
- [ ] Bin Liners

Food

Any food you carry should where possible be in small quantities. Throughout the route there are many towns, villages and corner shops to buy food. The areas that are more remote are in Scotland as well as along the A30 in Cornwall. These I have mentioned in other sections of the book.

Carry enough food/snacks for the days when you are cycling in the remote areas. Generally there are fuel stations where you can buy snacks and occasionally you pass truck stops or roadside cafes. These places provide cheap meals and drinks, which I found very welcoming as I progressed along the route.

Try to eat food for energy e.g. fruit, nut type chocolate bars and when stopping for a full meal eat rice, pasta, wholemeal bread or jacket potato. Plan your route to arrive near villages and/or food stops if possible, but have some spare food with you just in case this is difficult.

I did not take a stove with me, due to the space and weight. My main meals were purchased in places like Co-op or Tesco cafés, bar meals and roadside cafes/truck stops.

Things not to take

It is easy to get all your things ready to take but the fun starts when you try to get it all into your panniers and bags. You need to be strict and leave out all the extras. Work on the principle that ounces and grammes turn into pounds and kilograms. Instead of taking a large bottle of sun cream for example, take a smaller one. Take enough toothpaste only for the time you expect to take to complete the end to end. Use this method for all your things you wish to take.

Should you do this and be miserly in your quantities, you may even have room to spare in your panniers to enable some of those 'luxuries' to be included.

Daily Stops

You can always cycle shorter distances each day and fit your schedule to where the B&Bs are. Advantage is that you will have a good bed and shower at night, but the disadvantage is that you will often have to cycle generally 2 - 4 miles into a village to find one, and then back the next day to the main route. This will increase and prolong your overall journey. The other disadvantages of staying in a B&B are that you will probably get a late start each morning and of course the cost of staying there compared to camping. It is worth considering using B&Bs one night and camping the next.

When I cycled, I stayed on the main route all the time but noted where the villages were that I would pass through and I tried to ensure I reached a B&B before nightfall. Sometimes there were no B&Bs around at all and others were full so I used my small tent in a nearby field. It is important to carry at least a 'bivi' bag for emergency, but you may prefer to take a small tent and camp more often.

When in a B&B, have a good breakfast to get you off to a fine start. When camping, I had a tin of cold beans or mackerel to keep me going each morning. Don't forget the small things to eat in between to give you a constant supply of energy.

Lunchtime or evening, I always tried to have one hot meal a day, whether a pub lunch or evening meal. Truck stops are very good places to rest, with good prices and food. Packs of sandwiches sufficed in between or evenings when in the B&B or camping, unless the B&B did hot evening meals, which were always welcome.

Remember to get off your cycle and move limbs regularly to keep the circulation going and stretch legs etc. This will help you stay supple and keep the stiffness away, especially from the bottom, hands and wrists.

TRAINING PLAN

To complete a venture like this requires a good level of fitness and stamina. Start your training with short rides and build up over a few months to cycling up to 90 miles a day over a three-day period.

You will find that any extra training you can do in the gym, swimming or jogging will all help, but do not overdo it. Building the leg muscles with a variety of exercises is the important part. It is all about getting the quadriceps, calf and lower ankle and the shoulders and hips into shape, as well as raising your lactate threshold for this long and arduous task.

You cannot beat the actual practice on the cycle itself especially with full panniers on. I trained without any extra weight on the cycle and was amazed how hard it was to cycle when I put on the full panniers. This I think is the most important point.

The two weeks before you go ease off on the training and rest more. Use the time to sort out your clothing and equipment. Check the cycle for loose nuts and bolts, handlebars and wheels and ensure you have plenty of high visibility clothing.

Photo 4. The View and Paths Around the Lands End Complex

SAFETY CONSIDERATIONS

The entire route is mainly on road, with the occasional section on cycle tracks where possible. The roads can be extremely busy in some areas, especially in rush hour traffic. It is very important to be aware of the hazards a cyclist poses to the unsuspecting driver.

Try if possible to make an early start around 5.30am or earlier if you can, depending upon the time of year. This may be difficult though if you are staying in a B&B as it often results in a later start. It will help you to cover some distance before the traffic builds up on the roads, apart from having cleaner air to breathe. In your planning, take note where the busy sections or more populated sections are and try to avoid them during rush hour.

It is important to wear bright reflective or high visibility clothing, similar to what the police wear. Bright clothing helps you to be seen and could ultimately save your life. I wore bright yellow shorts and vest most of the time in hot weather or when cycling on winding roads.

Take a good set of lights for front and back of the cycle. Do not cycle on roads in darkness, as it can be dangerous, use the daylight for cycling. It is illegal to cycle at night without lights and a rear reflector. To see is to be seen!

Light for the front of a cycle comes in two kinds. A good LED light, which will give light so you can be seen, but not necessarily to cycle long distance in the dark, and larger (and heavier) battery powered lights. The battery lights are more powerful so you could cycle in the dark, but the disadvantage is that the packs are generally heavy so it all adds to the overall weight you are carrying. It is wise to cycle by day and sleep by night.

Carry some identity with you and contact friends or relatives regularly to report your position. I found it very helpful to carry a mobile telephone with me. It can be recharged if you stay in a B&B. In some areas there is no reception e.g. mountainous areas and some other places. You can also use your phone if you need to phone a TIC for a B&B or other information.

It is recommended you take a spare inner tube for the journey as well as a puncture repair kit. If you are unlucky enough to have a puncture, you do not want to be spending a lot of time on a grass verge by a busy road repairing it.

Depending on the time of year you may need midge cream or sun cream. I found these necessary, cycling in August, and especially going through Scotland, as the midges were plentiful and it was hot! A good covering of midge cream and I was thankfully saved from bites. Sunglasses may be of benefit, but that is another item to carry. They did however stop flies getting into my eyes and the wind making them water.

Take plenty of drinks with you and refill where you can, even by knocking on someone's door. If you sweat a lot you may need an extra water bottle. Sometimes it is quite a distance between habitations, particularly in Scotland. Eat little and often during the day to keep your energy levels up, having a good meal in the evening. Carry enough food for the section, and plan ahead but do not take too much as you have to carry it.

Take a good supply of first aid items with you, particularly elastic stockings for leg problems and knee/ankle supports. A tube of anti-histamine cream for nettle or wasp stings is very useful as I found out. A supply of anti-inflammatory tablets can be of use if you are accustomed to swelling of various joints.

Summarising this section, the most important points to consider are the wearing of bright clothing, having plenty of water to avoid dehydration and knee/ankle supports.

HEALTH ON ROUTE

Your health on the journey is important so you need to devote some time on route to it.

Head

Always wear your cycle helmet. Accidents can happen in the most unlikely places. Because you are travelling so many miles in a short time, there is more risk of accidents due to complacency.

Hands & Wrists

These areas can suffer major damage on an expedition like this. Numbness in the hands is especially a problem as well as wrists aching. These are caused by the pressing of the hands for long periods on the handlebars and the vibration through the cycle as you go over bumps and potholes. It is the nerves that get damaged and it can take up to six months for them to recover!

Check your body position on the bike so you are not exerting undue pressure on your hands. Try multiple seat and handlebar positions to ensure less weight on hands when cycling. Ensure you have gel gloves, as this is essential to help absorb the pressure. If possible try to have moulded or softer shock absorbing grips put on the handlebars before you leave. At regular intervals and if safe to do so, take one hand off the handlebars and move it around, moving fingers as well to keep good circulation going. Move hands around to different positions on the handlebar during the ride.

Neck & Back

Before starting, do some warm up exercises to move the neck and back. Stop at suitable times on route to stretch and keep the circulation moving by brief exercises. Problems in these areas are often caused by over use but may be to other causes. A massage often helps, and on route there are some B&Bs who will give a massage.

Bottom

Riding for several days with a numb or sore bottom can be painful. The long days sitting on the saddle does have an effect, but this can be reduced a lot. Again like the above, adjustment to saddle height can help lessen the pain, but this needs to be done in conjunction with the other cycle adjustments outlined above.

When I cycled both times, I used a gel seat with a gel cover on top of it. In other words double gel! I did not get any discomfort until the sixth day. To try to alleviate this, I stopped regularly and moved around, rubbing the bottom to get the circulation moving again. Generally it seemed to work.

Each evening when you stop, wash between your legs and ensure it is dried properly. Wear padded cycling shorts, which can absorb the bumps and pressure also. Try to wear clean shorts each day or at least every other day, if clothing limitations apply. There is no magical solution other than try these recommendations and hope they work for you as they did for me.

Eyes

You are liable, depending on the month you go, to get the sun in the south and the midges in the north. June to September is the months for the midges. Sunglasses help to keep the wind out of your eyes and deflect the flies/midges from them so it may be wise to take some.

Ears

If you are prone to earache, particularly where the wind whistles round your ears causing discomfort then you can do two things.

- Take some cotton wool to put in your ears to stop the cold
- Wear a sweatband over your ears and brow, again preventing the cold wind from getting in.

YOUR BICYCLE

The cycle you choose is the most important item you take. If you experience problems with your cycle then the whole expedition could be at risk. On an expedition of this length, undertaken in a mixture of weather and usually carrying more weight and equipment than you normally would, your cycle is tested to its limits.

Choosing a cycle

There are all kinds of vehicles you could use to go from end to end, from go-carts to prams, but here we will look at the bicycle. There are three main types of cycle you could choose from: -

- **The Racing Bike**
- **The Hybrid Bike**
- **The Mountain Bike**

The racing bike is fine if you are going to go for a fast time and you have got support to feed you and carry your clothing etc and go on ahead to book the B&B or set up tent. By taking care on the roads to ensure the narrow tyres don't go down ruts and holes in the road then you can use this generally lightweight bike to get a good time.

The mountain bike is not really suitable unless you are going to do some off road cycling on route. In this book, where we are discussing the fastest/shortest route by road, then I would advise against a mountain bike. The tyres are wide which creates more drag to slow you down. The absence of mudguards will not help in those torrential downpours we can sometimes experience.

The hybrid bike is the best for the following reasons
The wheels/tyres are in between the other two, giving a descent grip on the road and more robust than a racing bike.
It usually has mudguards to help deflect any surface water etc.
The general frame, seat and overall nature of the bike is more robust than the racing bike but not as heavy and cumbersome as the mountain bike.

Generally the more you pay out the better bike you can get. This is true, but there is no need to spend vast sums. Do not buy a £50.00 all shining bike from a local shop as more often than not, the wheels will buckle or some other mishap will occur as soon as you hit that pothole! All that glitters is not gold!

Look for a bike with some street 'cred'. A name that is talked about or better still enquire from the cycle shops what the best buy is for your money.

Accessories

Accessories that should be included on your bicycle are mudguards, padded grips on the handlebars and toe clips to help keep feet on the pedals. Panniers on the sides at the rear, one on the front handlebars and if needed panniers on the front wheel. A most welcome addition to the bike is a gel seat and a gel cover on top of that. Your bottom may just last out until the end before becoming numb with the addition of both of these!

Don't forget the water bottles (2 at least) and a small tool bag that fits between the cycle frame to put the essential tools etc. in. A cycle lock is a must if you are leaving your cycle out overnight, and make it a good one. Throughout the expedition, I was never far away from my only means of transport. Lastly a waterproof map stand/case to fix on the handlebars to put this book in and the relevant map sections previously mentioned.

Things that can go wrong

There are numerous events that could affect your journey but below are the things that are most likely to happen to your cycle.

Tyre puncture – Take at least one spare inner tube and a repair kit as well as any spanners etc to remove/tighten vital parts.

Buckled wheel rim – Caused by going over potholes in the road. Ensure the wheels you have on the cycle are of reasonable quality.

Brake blocks wearing down or coming off completely – Start with new blocks and thoroughly check before you leave, as there are a lot of hills to descend.

Handlebars getting slack or out of alignment – This can happen with vibration or going over potholes. Ensure the handlebars are fully secured and aligned before you leave.

Panniers or front handlebar bag touching wheels or a moving part – Although they may seem a good fit initially, once you fill them, the weight and movement can often dislodge them and this can ultimately delay you on your journey.

Chain coming off or breaking – This can happen if the chain is too slack, too tight or not lubricated. Ensure the chain is fitted properly and have a trial run before leaving to see if it is fitted correctly. If unsure, visit a cycle shop to have it checked. Keep the chain links thoroughly lubricated and take a chain tool for emergency, if you can use one.

Lights – Although it is not advisable to cycle at night, you should still have lights that operate. Insert new batteries before you start and ensure lights operate correctly.

Slack wheels – If not secured well before you leave, again the potholes will loosen them and you may fall off!

Broken spokes – Due to the increased pressure of carrying a load. Take some spare spokes and the spoke key if you know how to repair it, otherwise get to the nearest cycle shop. I did not have any problem with spokes on two end to ends, but it could happen.

From all the above points, the cycle shops tell me that buckled wheel rims are the main problem due to inferior metal and rims. As far as quality is concerned, you get what you pay for.

Other Important Considerations

- Cycle clips if you have trousers that could get caught in the chain.

- A cycle helmet is essential for safety.

- A cycle raincoat/cape is essential to protect you from the elements.

- Gel gloves are essential if you don't want numb hands because of the constant pressure on the nerves of the hands pressing on the handlebars.

- A clear waterproof plastic pocket or tray that sits on the handlebars or on the front carrying bag is helpful so you can put map and/or route description in.

- A good cycle lock.

- Reflective/high visibility jacket/shorts, stripes on other items. **Be safe, be seen!**

Photo 5. See and be Seen!

PUBLICITY & SPONSORSHIP

With events of this kind it is not just the challenge of completing the journey but to raise sponsorship for a worthwhile cause. There are many charities that will produce sponsorship forms for you to circulate among family/friends etc. This can sometimes bring in thousands of pounds for the charity of your choice.

An alternative to the traditional way of sponsorship is guessing your finishing time. You could charge people for guessing when you will finish in days, hours, minutes and seconds from the start line to the finish line. It is of course pure guesswork.

Asking companies for donations is worth considering especially if you are having a support vehicle and you are prepared to advertise their company on the vehicle. They may even buy your equipment for you, provide the vehicle, or fuel for the journey.

Publicity in your local area will help with sponsorship. Any unusual method of travelling between the two points may warrant publicity in national magazines or on TV. Local radio stations can be contacted to give live interviews on route, but set this up before you leave home.

You may find you can get support bandages etc or other items you may be likely to use sponsored by chemist shops or companies.

When I cycled I put on a t-shirt with Lands End to John O'Groats on it. I was amazed how generous people were with donations, free tea and food etc., particularly at roadside mobile cafes. If you can also put the name of a charity on the same t-shirt then you should do even better in raising money for your charity.

One final word on sponsorship/publicity, you can be as successful as your imagination and determination will allow you. Think about how much you want to raise and what clothing, equipment or fuel you can get sponsored, then set about your task with enthusiasm.

FINANCIAL CONSIDERATIONS

A challenge such as this can make a sizeable hole in your pocket if you do not plan it properly. Initially you need to purchase your main equipment, bicycle, trainers, panniers, tent and clothing if you do not already have them. You may be able to get them sponsored either by a local shop or business or from a national supplier. This may however be difficult as national suppliers get hundreds of letters asking for equipment, so unless you can offer something different on your cycle ride, then there is often not much chance of getting anything from them.

Once you have your equipment you need to plan how to get to Lands End. Haulage Company's have a network of contacts and may be able to help, so make enquiries early. There are train services to Penzance and you are able to take a cycle on them, again enquire early. You then need to cycle the 12 miles to Lands End to start your expedition. On reaching John O'Groats, you have to cycle 17miles back to Wick, where you can get a train to other parts of the UK.

Assuming you are travelling without support, your biggest cost will be B&Bs or camping, along with food. B&Bs can be as much as £40.00 in some places, especially in the south and £20.00 near John O'Groats but generally prices were around the £25.00 - £30.00 mark. I recommend carrying a small lightweight tent or a bivi bag. There are places where there are no B&Bs on route or they may be full and you may need to sleep outdoors as I did some nights.

Should you have a support team then the costs involved with that can be substantial. I travelled without support until the final 40miles of the expedition. This is not a problem as long as you can wash your clothes and get them dried. I attached mine to the straps on my cycle to dry, which was very effective.

If you are lucky enough to have someone with an estate car, you may be able to travel light with the car nearby all day and at night, sleep in the estate car where there is enough room to sleep. The cost of the estate car accompanying you would more than be met from the saving in B&B costs alone each night.

The above is a resumé of the main financial considerations but work out your own costs giving consideration to the above points.

Photo 6. Leaving Penzance - The View of St. Michael's Mount

THE START/FINISH

Getting to the start

Lands End is situated in the south west of the UK. Rail links are available to the nearest town of Penzance, then you can cycle the 12 miles or so to the start at Lands End. It is worth enquiring whether the National bus network will transport your cycle to Penzance. Alternatively a car, friends to drive you there and a cycle rack should do the trick.

If you are intending to travel to the start by train, you need to make a reservation and obtain tickets for yourself and your cycle before travelling. On most trains, the number of cycles able to be carried is limited. This applies to/from both ends. It should be free to make the reservation but things change quickly, so check in advance. National Rail has a leaflet with the details – 'cycling by train'. Ask at a station for it.

National Express operates coach services to Penzance and to/from Inverness. Cycles do need to be packed flat though and in a case or large bag, possibly cling filmed may be acceptable.

Beside the entrance to the Lands End complex is a start/finish line (photo 1), and there is a similar line at John O'Groats outside the hotel (photo 2). You could not leave Lands End without a photograph at the signpost (photo 3) to record your start and equally at the signpost at John O'Groats to record your finish.

Lands End is a tourist attraction and has many visitors. If you have a support vehicle with you, entry to the car park is free if they mention to the attendant they are doing support. Inside the complex you can purchase food and drinks as well as view the attractions, which are free to 'End to Enders' starting or finishing there.

You will see the start line ahead as you reach the main building. Go to the post room, just nearby the 'Miles of Memories' attraction as you enter, to collect your form and have it stamped. If arriving at night, go to the hotel reception nearby.

John O'Groats is situated in the far north east of Scotland. Trains connect from Thurso and from Wick to many towns and cities throughout the UK. Wick is the nearest to John O'Groats being only 17 miles. After you complete your expedition, cycle to one of these places to connect with transport back to your hometown. Cyclists have had problems in the past actually getting their bike back from John O'Groats, so as soon as you know the finish date of your journey, book the train or coach to return. In some cases it has taken a week to get on a train with a bike! Again, buses from Wick may transport you and your cycle back home. (see useful addresses in appendix)

Arriving in John O'Groats, you have a beautiful view of the nearby islands. The air is clean and fresh usually with a slight wind blowing most of the time. There is a tourist information centre and a café as well as a collection of small gift shops. The hotel on the front has been closed for a number of years and awaiting refurbishment although the bar on the ground floor is open.

The passenger ferry leaves from the small harbour nearby, stopping off at the islands. The last house in Scotland (photo 12) is nearby the harbour. In here you have your form stamped to complete your expedition. Should the shop be closed then you can go to the bar in the hotel a short distance away. (See section on "Getting the Form Stamped").

Try to finish during normal daytime hours as transport back to Wick is daytime only and the café and shops are closed in the evenings.

GETTING YOUR FORM STAMPED

To qualify for a certificate or other souvenir to mark your achievement, you need to provide some proof of your journey. Both the CTC and the Lands End/John O'Groats Club have a form, which you can complete and get stamped along the route as you progress.

Generally local shops or a fuel garage will stamp it. Post offices can be awkward, as they are not supposed to use their official stamp for this kind of thing. Generally, every 50 to 100 miles, stop off somewhere and get the shop to stamp and sign the form as proof you passed through.

If you cannot get the form signed/stamped, then cash point withdrawal receipts are accepted, as are general receipts for food in shops on way. Generally most things are accepted as long as they have an address on them and date to verify your journey, so don't worry too much and just collect your receipts on the way, including any B&B receipts.

When you get back, send proofs and any money required to obtain certificates, badges, t-shirts etc. it is nice to look back and remember your cycle expedition from one end of the country to the other with a souvenir to mark your journey.

Photo 7. Looking Across the Severn Bridge

PRACTICAL ADVICE

- Ensure you can understand and read a map well enough before you start and the maps used are up to date showing current roads

- Try to plan your night stops to coincide with the B&Bs shown in this book or at villages

- Plan a training programme; gradually increase distance and body strength

- Ensure clothing is bright or has reflective stripes on it

- Ensure you wear a cycle helmet

- Ensure all food, clothing and other items carried are kept to a minimum

- If possible, have someone to meet you on your journey with a change of clothing to save washing

- Eat a well balanced diet that is carbohydrate rich

- Use every opportunity to replenish food and drink stocks. Drink regularly and expect to drink about 500ml per hour

- Eat little and often and drink plenty throughout the day. Eat something every 1-2 hours, which will give you a constant supply of energy

- Alternate between B&Bs and bivi bag/tent if possible for a bath one day and an early start the next

- Be aware of traffic at all times in front and from behind

- Keep details on your person of next of kin, medical information, blood group etc. in case of accident

- Ensure you carry the minimum repair kit, which is spare inner tubes, tyre levers and pump

QUESTIONS YOU MAY ASK

How long will it take to cycle and how many miles is it?

The distance is approximately 910 miles, some say 910 – 960 miles but as far as I know, the shortest distance is 874 miles on motorways etc. Allowing for the by-roads and winding minor roads it is at least 900 miles.

It will normally take between 6 - 15 days but it depends if you cycle into villages off route for accommodation and the weather, muscle/hand problems, weight of cycle overall including panniers, any support and speed to name but a few. If you do it in less time then you are fit!

Are there any areas I can get lost on?

Generally the route is well signposted and if you take the route sections of map and a copy of the route described in this book then you should not have a problem. You do not need a compass. Look for the road numbers and places, if you are not sure then ask.

Is the route safe?

I found the route generally safe apart from the busy roads and the winding country lanes where you obviously have to take extra care and try to always wear some high visibility clothing. As regards general safety, the route is no problem but always be cautious. I never had any problems on my expedition anywhere.

Which were the areas that presented most problems when cycling?

The main problems I encountered were not seeing any shops where I could buy food, drinks or other items. There was not even a pub where I could obtain a meal. This was mainly from Aberfeldy up to Inverness, and along the A9 road. The section from Gretna Green to Lanark was also short of shops, as was the A30 from Penzance to Okehampton. If you needed to purchase food etc, you would need to cycle into the villages you pass.

The other area that presented problems was around Tiverton and Crediton in Devon because of the short undulating hills. Just before Queenswood Country Park near Hereford there is a long steep ascent and there is also the daunting Shap Fell to climb between Penrith and Kendal. Around Berriedale and generally through northeast Scotland there are many steep and undulating roads.

Are there plenty of B&Bs on route?

No, there are not many throughout the route. When starting, there are plenty in Penzance area and again in John O'Groats and Wick when finishing and generally in most villages through Scotland. There are few B&Bs between Wishaw and Stirling. Along the A9 there are few B&Bs unless you turn into a village.

Depending on the time of year you may find the B&Bs are full, especially in July/August. Cycling along the A30 in Cornwall there was none so either be prepared to go into a village nearby or to wild camp in a field just off the road. Between Whitchurch and Preston there was only one that I saw and between Crawford and Gretna there are only two or three B&Bs. New B&Bs open as do others close, so you may come across others on your journey.

The alternative is to telephone the TIC's (see appendix) throughout the route to obtain current B&B lists and pre-book all the way. The danger in doing this is that it is a long way and anything can happen with injuries, tiredness, punctures, mechanical failure, the weather and overall fitness that may slow you down and prevent you from reaching the B&B you pre-booked.

I tried to plan to be near a village on route in the evening but it did not always work out and if there are no B&Bs for 60 miles then you have no option but to sleep outside or cycle off route into a village.

Is the whole route on road and are there any cycle lanes?

Yes, it is the shortest route by road with only two small exceptions to avoid long steep hills or winding dangerous bends. There are cycle lanes intermittently on roads throughout the route but the main cycle tracks are on the A9 heading to Inverness where you can, in parts, be totally off the main road but cycling close by it.

What type of roads do I cycle on?

There are many A roads and some B roads and when in the far reaches of Scotland, you have some single track roads with passing places!

There is a section of dual carriageway as you pass Camborne and Redruth then a long section to Okehampton with shorter sections throughout the route. A margin at the side gives protection along the A30. At no point on the route do you cycle on motorways.

In Scotland there are longer stretches of dual carriageway on the A9 with sections of cycle track. The dual carriageways tend to have a cycle lane or at least a margin down the left side with a white line, where you have some safety on the inside of the line. You should not find much problem as long as you can be seen easily and you are sensible, and not riding two abreast on narrow or fast moving roads.

What is the general state of the roads for cycling on?

The roads throughout are generally good but on any road you will always come across the occasional pothole or severely worn sections. This applies throughout the route. Advice is to keep your eyes on the road to avoid the potholes and ruts. I only came off my bike once and that was when I caught a kerb in Bridgewater, but it can happen anytime to anyone.

What tools etc specifically should I take for the venture?

Below is a list of recommended cycle tools:

- Relevant allen keys
- Spanners or adjustable one
- Spare spokes and spoke key
- Puncture repair kit
- Spare inner tube
- Tyre levers
- Spare brake/gear cable
- Small tin of WD40
- Chain key

- Inflator
- Cycle lights for front/rear
- Cycle helmet
- Screwdrivers as required
- Spare valve
- A few assorted cable ties
- Brake blocks
- Spare batteries for headlamp/back light
- Cycle lock

Photo 8. A Last look Back at Hereford

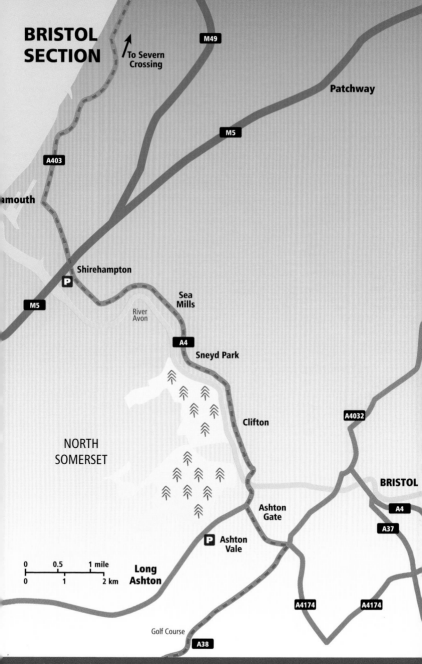

BRISTOL SECTION

To Severn Crossing

M49

Patchway

M5

A403

...amouth

M5

Shirehampton

P

Sea Mills

River Avon

A4

Sneyd Park

Clifton

A4032

NORTH SOMERSET

BRISTOL

A4

Ashton Gate

A37

P Ashton Vale

0   0.5   1 mile
0   1   2 km

Long Ashton

A4174   A4174

Golf Course

A38

HEREFORD SECTION

Theatre

Hereford
United F.C.

Mediaeval
Museum

A49

Livestock
Market

A438

A438

H Victoria
Eye
Hospital

Cider
Museum

Cathedral

i

River Wye

Hereford
Rugby
Club

Greyfriars
Bridge

A49

Swimming
Baths

0				250yds
0				250m

THE ROUTE

The route is generally well signposted throughout so you should not have much problem. I would advise you to have a list of the relevant road numbers in front of you on your cycle handlebars so you can check without having to take out your map each time you want to check the route.

In the route described below, I will not mention every twist and turn but concentrate on the road numbers, as these are mostly signposted. I will mention notable points on some parts of the route to help guide you through those parts. This route section is also abbreviated to cut out irrelevant words and the text has been enlarged so you can read it from a distance on the cycle.

1. Starting at the start line outside the Lands End main building (photo 1), cycle along the road passing through a number of small villages on the winding, undulating A30 road. Keep on main road to descend a hill after 12 miles, arriving at the Tesco roundabout on outskirts of Penzance.

2. Next section approx. 6 miles to Hale roundabout still on A30 with both 2-way and dual carriageway sections. Cross several roundabouts with St. Michael's Mount off to your right (photo 6). Continue on same road passing Cambourne and monuments on hillside off to your right. Continue to the far side of Bodmin.

3. Continue towards Bodmin passing Blackwater then Indian Queens, on the dual carriageway. Approaching Bodmin, cycle a further 26 miles by-passing Bodmin then passing the turning to Jamaica Inn before arriving at Launceston outskirts on A30.

4. Stay on A30, dual carriageway, to B3260 turn off to Okehampton centre. The road is not so busy now as you pass through the high street in Okehampton. At far side of town, turn left onto the B3215 towards Crediton for approx. 5 miles before leading onto the A3072 then onto the A377 taking you into Crediton.

5. The road between Crediton and Tiverton is very undulating. Follow signs to Tiverton on the A3072 then A396, turning right to avoid town centre. Pass over a series of roundabouts taking you to A361 dual carriageway. Cycle on this road for 7 miles to J27 of the M5.

6. A small restaurant is nearby as you cross to the A38 2-way road initially ascending from the roundabout then on to the village of Wellington. You now have a 5 mile stretch to Taunton. On entering, follow the one-way system to the far side

of the town then at a large roundabout, follow A38 signs towards North Petherton and Bridgwater, turning left at lights on dual carriageway to cross the canal.

7. This section is reasonably flat as you pass through North Petherton then into Bridgwater. Stay on A38 following signs for Highbridge then pass through a series of small villages, follow signs for Bristol or airport. Pass Bristol Airport on the undulating road and descend gradually into Bristol on A38.

8. Follow signs towards city centre then as you cross the river Avon, turn left onto the A4 going under the Clifton Suspension Bridge towards Avonmouth 5 miles ahead. Stay on A4 going under the M5 to the large roundabout at Avonmouth then onto A403 towards the Severn Bridge (2nd crossing).

9. Pass the 1st Severn Crossing then just before reaching the motorway over the 2nd Severn Bridge, turn left on a minor road then right, taking you past the bridge maintenance depot on a cycle path to emerge on the cycle track on the left side of the bridge (photo 7). Cyclists can cross free so continue to the far side

then descend a path on the left, turning right under the motorway at the far side then left up a cycle track, now on the right side.

10. Ascend to the roundabout following signs A48 Chepstow then A466 to Monmouth. Pass Chepstow racecourse and continue on winding and mainly ascending road passing Tintern Abbey and Llandogo before reaching Monmouth. Cross the A40 into Monmouth and follow the road through town on the A466 towards Hereford.

11. Stay on A466 then when it merges with A49, turn left cycling into Hereford. Cross main bridge in Hereford then follow signs, right at the roundabout then further on turning left still on the A49 towards Leominster. 6 miles north of Hereford is a steep ascent to Queenswood Country Park on top of the hill with a steep descent on far side. Approaching Leominster, stay on by-pass still on A49 to Ludlow.

12. Approaching Ludlow, turn left on the minor road into Ludlow, go directly through town to rejoin A49 on north side. Continue on A49 past Craven Arms and Church Stretton until you reach

the ring road around Shrewsbury. Cross ring road cycling straight through town following signs A49 Whitchurch. Stay on A49 to Whitchurch and on meeting the ring road, continue as before directly through town centre. Rejoin A49 on north side again.

13. Next part is through a flatter area but with few facilities until Warrington. Stay on A49, passing Weaverham then cross M56 before arriving at Stockton Heath then into Warrington. Just before the town centre in Warrington, cross a large bridge then at the large roundabout there, which is usually very busy, turn right following signs for Newton Le Willows and M62.

14. At the M62, cross over it still on A49 and cycle directly to Newton Le Willows then Ashton–in–Mackerfield. Continue to Wigan on A49 and stay on this road through Standish and Coppull. You should see M6 off to your left as you reach Charnock Richard. Follow signs now for Euxton and Preston, staying on A49 until you see signs for A6 into Preston.

15. Cycle along a stretch of dual carriageway as you enter Preston. The road ascends

passing the park on your right still on the A6. The road now is flat for around 30 miles leaving Preston, going under the M55 and heading for Garstang on A6. Turn off to Garstang; it is shorter and quicker to head into Garstang and through to far side, picking up the A6 again on far side.

16. You now have a 12 mile section into Lancaster. At the roundabout as you enter Lancaster, follow the one-way system round the city, crossing the river bridge and staying on A6 to Carnforth. Again, stay on A6 following signs for Hale, Milnthorpe or Kendal. You emerge on the A590 dual carriageway and turn right then after a short distance left on A591 taking you to Kendal.

17. After 3 miles, bear right onto the A6 directly into Kendal. Cycle through the high street and stay on A6 following signs for Shap and Penrith. Once you leave Kendal there is a gradual ascent to the top of Shap Fell. It can be a very inhospitable area in adverse weather conditions, so be well prepared. After crossing the summit, there is a long descent on the far side still on A6 taking you into Shap Village.

18. From Shap, continue on the undulating A6 road passing Hackthorpe and Lowther then eventually emerging at the roundabout on A66 just before Penrith. Cross with care, cycling into Penrith centre and stay on A6 following signs for Plumpton and Carlisle. This is a quiet undulating road where you can make good progress to Carlisle.

19. Arriving at the roundabout at M6, J.42, continue on same road into Carlisle centre. Follow the one-way system and signs for Gretna or Dumfries A7, B7076. You come to a roundabout at far side of City then cross the bridge. Cycle a further 2 miles on A7 to another roundabout over the M6 at J.44 and turn left onto B7076 heading northwest (new in 2009).

20. This new 'service road' on the left side is approx. 7 miles and runs parallel with the new section of motorway, and is the main border crossing into Scotland. Cycle along here to a small roundabout into Gretna. Go straight across then into Gretna Green. Look for cycle signs and pick up the B7076 to Kirkpatrick Fleming.

21. You are now on a quiet road with long stretches, running right up to Crawford, parallel with the A74M motorway. There are some small villages but very few shops. Continue on through Kirtlebridge then Ecclefechan on B7076. When you reach the roundabout near Lockerbie, you can either continue north or cycle the short distance into Lockerbie where there are cafes and a variety of shops.

22. Continuing from Lockerbie, stay on this somewhat isolated road with few amenities and pass Beatock. Cycle into Crawford where there is limited accommodation. A short distance further is Abington where there is a shop. Cycle through, then at the roundabout at far side, turn right following signs for Roberton and Lanark A73. Pass through Roberton staying on A73.

23. Continue through Lanark town centre where there are many shops and stay on A73 through to Carluke then outskirts of Wishaw, passing over a number of roundabouts in between. The next 4 miles on A73 takes you to Chapelhall as you pass over the M8. A further 3 miles takes you into Airdrie. Stay on A73 for approx. 2 miles north of Airdrie then look

for B8039 turning right on minor road to Luggiebank then onto the B8011 into Cumbernauld Village.

24. The B8011 crosses the A80 dual carriageway onto the B816 to Castlecary. Once through the village, turn onto the A80 for ½ mile to the start of the M80 then off onto the A803 following signs for Denny and Stirling. The road runs parallel with M80 as you cycle through this built up area of Denny then Dunipace on the A872. After cycling through a section of agricultural land, you cross over the M9, follow signs for Bannockburn and St. Ninians now joining the A9 and passing Bannockburn Visitors Centre on your left.

25. Continue into Stirling centre and cross a bridge over the river following signs to Bridge of Allan. You pass near Wallace monument as you cycle through a shopping area leaving Stirling, then cross a bridge into Bridge of Allan. Stay on A9 to Dunblane 3miles further and pass through the town to join the B8033 for ¾ mile to the A9 dual carriageway. Turn right here onto the A9 for 3½ miles to the turn off to Greenloaning on the A822.

26. Stay on this road for approx. 12 miles passing through Braco then Muthill on this sometimes hilly, winding, isolated road to Crieff. In Crieff there are shops and many B&Bs. Cycle up the hill in town, then turn right into the main high street.

Continue through on the A85 following Perth signs then turn left following signs for Aberfeldy on A822. This winding, undulating and isolated road stretches 14 miles and passes through Amulree before turning left onto A826 into Aberfeldy, a further 9 miles.

27. There are shops in Aberfeldy before you cycle into the more remote region of the highlands. In the town centre follow signs for Weem and Tummel Bridge and cross the humpback bridge over the river onto the B846 minor road. Cycle this isolated road into Tummel Bridge passing occasional houses on route. Entering Tummel Bridge, the power station is on left with good views over the river area opposite.

28. Stay on the B846 bearing left towards Kinloch Rannoch then after approx. ½ mile, turn right onto a very minor road which ascends for approx. 3 miles by a forest

to emerge near Trinafour. Turn right into Trinafour then left in the village towards the A9 at Dalnacardoch. This is on a one-track road over the open moor. You emerge on the busy A9 where you turn left.

29. The road now has a cycle-way intermittently along the A9 for a considerable distance. Cycle on the cycle-way where possible, or on the A9 where necessary, right to Inverness and beyond for over 100 miles. The wind can be strong along the A9 as you pass over Drumochter summit then further on passing turn off for Dalwhinnie. Further ahead pass turn off for Newtonmore and Kingussie, cycling towards Aviemore through some spectacular scenery, still on A9.

30. Pass the turning into Aviemore, unless you need food or accommodation, and continue on A9 passing over Slochd summit then past Tomatin and Services there (a good stopping off place). Ascending gently towards the hills overlooking Inverness on A9, you come to Daviot Village then soon after a tourist information on your left. From here it is downhill to Inverness and the main bridge over the Moray Firth.

31. Inverness has many B&Bs and shops 1½ miles off to the left at the bridge, otherwise pass the football stadium on your right and cross the impressive bridge ahead (photo 9), still on A9. You are now on the Black Isle heading for Tore roundabout approx. 7 miles ahead along this busy dual carriageway. If you turn left just across the bridge into North Kessock and cycle to the bottom of the road, there is a small supermarket on the left where you can purchase food etc.

32. Arriving at the Tore roundabout continue on the A9 towards Alness and Tain. After approx. 7 miles, cross the long bridge off the Black Isle and turn right at roundabout on the north side of the Cromarty Firth to eventually by-pass Alness. Continue on A9 to by-pass Tain unless stopping for food or B&B. On outskirts of Tain on A9 is the Glenmorangie distillery on the right, which is a good place to stop for a visit.

33. Descend the hill past the distillery to the roundabout beside the bridge crossing Dornoch Firth. Cross the long bridge still on A9 to by-pass Dornoch on route to Golspie, 6½ miles further. Cross another shorter bridge before cycling a further 5 miles into Golspie. There are some shops

here in the main street. You have now reached the final leg of your expedition. Leaving Golspie, you pass Dunrobin Castle on your right and continue to Brora where there are also shops and other amenities.

34. Cycle the long straight street through the town then through the villages of Loth (photo 11) and Portgower on this 21 mile section, descending the hill into Helmsdale. There are some shops there just off the main through road. Now you ascend the long winding road out of County of Sutherland. Next section is extremely hilly as you proceed on the winding road to Berriedale and the steepest hill on the journey.

35. Descend with care then ascend the winding road on far side. Further on you again come to a steep descent and ascent at Dunbeath. After this place, the remainder is generally flatter as you cycle to Latheron Wheel where there is a butchers and sweet shop on right just off the main road. At Latheron Village, leave the A9 and cycle by the coast on the A99 through a series of very small villages, Lybster, Occumster, Ulbster then Thrumster.

36. Arriving in Wick, cycle straight through, crossing the bridge in the centre and out at the far side, continuing on through the villages of Reiss, Keiss, Auckengill and Freswick, stay on A99 following signs to John O'Groats. You ascend a hillside before descending into John O'Groats.

37. Passing the Seaview Hotel, cycle to the harbour and cross the finish line beside the John O'Groats Hotel (photo 2). Look for the last house in Scotland (photo 12), where you register your journey. If the shop is closed, go to the John O'Groats Hotel to register there. Do not forget the photo at the signpost.

Congratulations on Completing Lands End to John O'Groats!

Photo 9. The Outskirts of Inverness & Frst Sign For John O'Groats

CARLISLE
SECTION

River Eden

A7

Cricket
Ground

Carlisle
Castle

A69

Market

i

Shopping
Centre

Bus
Station

River Caldew

Railway
Station

Cinema

A6

Retail
Park

0   400yds
0   400m

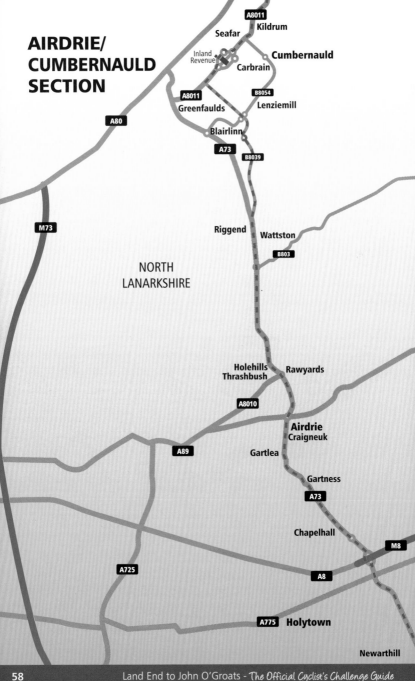

AIRDRIE/ CUMBERNAULD SECTION

A8011

Kildrum

Seafar

Inland Revenue

Cumbernauld

Carbrain

A8011

B8054

Greenfaulds

Lenziemill

A80

Blairlinn

A73

B8039

M73

Riggend

Wattston

B803

NORTH LANARKSHIRE

Holehills
Thrashbush

Rawyards

A8010

Airdrie
Craigneuk

A89

Gartlea

Gartness

A73

Chapelhall

M8

A725

A8

A775 **Holytown**

Newarthill

▲ Photo 10. One of the Steep Descents/Ascents Between Helmsdale & Dunbeath

▼ Photo 11. A Monument at the Side of the Road Near Loth

TO MARK THE PLACE NEAR WHICH
(ACCORDING TO SCROPE'S "ART OF DEERSTALKING")
THE LAST WOLF IN SUTHERLAND
WAS KILLED
BY THE HUNTER, POLSON,
IN OR ABOUT THE YEAR 1700,
THIS STONE WAS ERECTED BY
HIS GRACE THE DUKE OF PORTLAND, K.G.,
A.D. 1924.

CONCISE ROUTE SUMMARY

Lands End – A30
Penzance – A30
Bypass Cambourne – A30
Bypass Bodmin – A30
Launceston – B3260/A30
Okehampton – A3072/B3215
Crediton – A396/A3072
Tiverton – A38/A361
Taunton – A38
Bridgwater – A38
Bristol Airport – A38
Under Clifton Suspension Bridge – A4
Exit from Bristol – A4
Avonmouth – A403
Severn Bridge – cycle path on left side
Chepstow – A466
Monmouth – A49/A466
Hereford Town Centre – A49
Bypass Leominster – A49
Ludlow Town Centre – A49 – minor road
Craven Arms – A49
Church Stretton – A49
Shrewsbury Town Centre – A49
Whitchurch – A49
Weaverham – A49
Warrington – A49
Newton le Willows – A49
Ashton in- Makerfield – A49
Wigan – A49
Standish – A49
Bypass Leyland – A6/A49
Preston – A6
Garstang Village – A6/B6430
Lancaster – A6
Carnforth – A6
Kendal – A6
Shap – A6
Penrith – A6
Carlisle – A6
Gretna Green – B7076
Bypass Lockerbie – B7076
Bypass Moffat – B7076
Abington – A702
Roberton – A73
Lanark – A73
Carluke – A73

Chapelhall – A73
Airdrie – A73
Luggiebank – B8039
Cumbernauld Village – A8011
Castlecary – A9
Denny – A872
Dunipace – A872
Bannockburn – A9
Stirling – A9
Bridge of Allan – A9
Dunblane – A9
Greenloaning – A822
Muthill – A822
Crieff – A822
Amulree – A826
Aberfeldy – B846
Coshieville – B846
Tummel Bridge – minor road
Trinafour – minor road
Pass of Drumochter – A9
Dalnaspidal – A9
Bypass Dalwhinnie – A9
Bypass Kingussie – A9
Bypass Aviemore – A9
Slochd Summit – A9
Daviot – A9
Bypass Inverness – A9
North Kessock – A9
Tore roundabout – A9
Alness – A9
Tain – A9
Bypass Dornoch – A9
Golspie – A9
Brora – A9
Helmsdale – A9
Dunbeath – A9
Latheron – A9
Lybster – A99
Occumster – A99
Ulbster – A99
Thrumster – A99
Wick – A99
Keiss – A99
Auckengill – A99
Freswick – A99
John O'Groats A99

SUPPORT TEAM

Many people attempt this expedition each year; some have full support, some partial support, and others have none. Finding someone who has the time to spare to accompany you can be a problem, but if you can find someone it can make life a lot easier. Disadvantages are the time element, the cost of accommodation and fuel for the vehicle. Advantages are that you can stop when you have had enough and be picked up as well as receive regular drinks and food on route. Best vehicles for support are a van or an estate car, which you can sleep in each night, so choose wisely.

Mobile telephones are helpful for both the support and yourself so you can keep in contact. It is easy to miss each other, especially when going through large towns or encountering vehicle one-way systems.

Alternatively a supporter who can meet you once or twice on your journey with clean clothing and food etc. is helpful, but if you have support for the whole journey then you need to ask yourself the following questions: -

• How many people do you need to give adequate support?
  More people, more cost, more food, more sleeping provision.

• What sleeping arrangements have you for the support team, camping, B&B or in the back of a van or estate car for the night?

• Is the vehicle roadworthy and is it a thirsty one?

• Have you enough room in the vehicle for all clothing and equipment and is there room if you are sleeping in it.

• Are the support team or person equipped and trained to cope with map reading and first aid as well as long days driving?

• What facilities have you for washing/drying of everyone's clothes if needed?

FIRST AID

Should you be unfortunate to sustain an injury then it would be helpful if you have knowledge of basic first aid and a first aid kit with you.

Common Types of Injuries

- *Cuts and Grazes*
- *Ankle/Knee Swelling*
- *Blisters*
- *Hypothermia*
- *Sprained Ankle/Wrist*
- *Gashed Shins*
- *Bee/Nettle Stings*
- *Midge Bites*
- *Frozen Hands*

Individual First Aid Kit

- Adhesive Dressing
- Crepe Bandage
- Sterile Dressing
- Safety Pins
- Scissors
- Insect Repellent
- Blister Treatments
- Triangular Bandage
- Bandage
- Gauze/Lint
- Micropore
- SunCream

Hypothermia

If not prepared for the conditions or your clothing is not satisfactory, a combination of cold, wet, exhaustion and wind chill factor can cause the body core temperature to fall below 35°C resulting in hypothermia.

Ways of Preventing Hypothermia

- Build up body clothing in thin layers, adding on or taking off as necessary.
- Have suitable wind/waterproofs with you.
- Eat some food/hot drink or boiled sweets, which produce energy and heat during digestion.
- Wear a hat to insulate the head, and some gloves.

APPENDIX

Tourist Information Centres on Route

Penzance	01736 362207
Bodmin	01208 76616
Launceston	01566 772321
Okehampton	01837 53020
Crediton	01363 772006
Tiverton	01884 255827
Taunton	01823 336344
Bridgwater	01278 436438
Bristol	0845 4080474 Accommodation
Chepstow	01291 623772
Monmouth	01600 713899
Hereford	01432 268430
Leominster	01568 616460
Ludlow	01584 875053
Shrewsbury	01743 281200
Whitchurch	01948 664577
Warrington	01925 428585
Wigan	01942 825677
Preston	01772 253731
Kendal	01539 725758
Penrith	01768 867466
Carlisle	01228 625600
Gretna Green	01461 337834
Moffat	01683 220620
Lanark	01555 661661
Stirling	01786 475019
Crieff	01764 652578
Aberfeldy	01887 820276
Kingussie	01540 661297
Aviemore	01845 2255121
Daviot Wood	01845 2255121
Inverness	01845 2255121
Dornoch	01845 2255121
Wick	01845 2255121
John O'Groats	01845 2255121

Distances between Towns/Villages

To find a distance, read down then right.
e.g. Crediton to Tiverton = 14.4 miles

Lands End	
⇩	
Penzance ⇨	12
Hayle (A30)	8
Redruth (A30)	9.4
Victoria	24.9
Bodmin	8.6
Okehampton	42
Crediton	21
⇩	
Tiverton ⇨	14.4
North Petherton	31.9
Cross village	20.6
Bristol Airport	12.8
Severn Bridge (south east)	20.6
Tintern Abbey	8.7
Monmouth	14.5
Hereford	20.9
Leominster	15.7
Dorrington	33.4
Shrewsbury	7.5
Whitchurch	22.3
Stockton Heath	36.4
Warrington	4.3
Wigan	13.6
Standish Village	4.1
Euxton	9
Preston	8.1
Barton	5.6
Lancaster	20.8
Carnforth	7
Kendal	12.8
Shap	17.7
Hackthorpe	5.8
Carlisle Centre	26.6
Gretna	8.0
Kirkpatrick Fleming	4.6
Kirkpatrick Fleming	4.6
Ecclefechan	7.5
Crawford	43.2
Abington	3.6
Lanark	19.3
Carluke	5.9
Airdrie	13.8
Cumbernauld	6.6
Dunblane (south)	23.4
Braco	9.8
Crieff	10.8
Amulree	12.5
Trinafour	30.2
Drumochter Summit	14.3
Dalwhinnie (junction south)	4.8
Kingussie (junction north)	17.3
Aviemore (north junction)	14.9
Tomatin Services	14.2
Inverness Roundabout	17.4
Tore	7.6
Cromarty Firth Bridge	5.7
Alness	5.7
Dornoch Firth Bridge	18.1
Golspie	12.4
Brora Village (south end)	4.8
Helmsdale	12.7
Berriedale	9.2
Dunbeath	6.9
Latheronwheel	2.9
Thrumpster	14.4
Wick	4.8
Reiss	2.9
Keiss	4.9
Auckengill	2.7
Freswick	3.9
John O'Groats	3.1
	Total 900 Miles

Bed & Breakfast Selection

The following list of B&Bs has been chosen for reasonable prices, comfort and proximity to the cycling route. Most are directly on the route or within a short distance from it. They are not arranged in any order of priority other than route order. Many of those listed are accustomed to having 'End to Enders' staying and they can help and give advice when necessary. Some have "lock ups" for your cycle overnight.

You are advised to book in advance, especially during busy holiday periods. Some of the B&Bs listed can provide evening meals, please ask when booking. To obtain further B&Bs refer to the list of T.I.C's in the appendix for the areas you require. Please mention to the B&B that you have this book.

Penzance
Torwood House Hotel, Alexandra Road, Penzance. TR18 4LZ
Tel. 01736 360063
www.torwoodhousehotel.co.uk
email: lyndasowerby@aol.com

Redruth - Near railway station.
Mark & Marnie Webber, Lansdowne Guesthouse,
42 Clinton Rd, Redruth. TR15 2QE
Tel. 01209 216002
www.lansdowne-guesthouse.co.uk
email: enquiries@lansdowne-guesthouse.co.uk

Launceston
Glencoe Villa, 13 Race Hill, Launceston. PL15 9BB
Tel. 01566 775819
email: keigil.robinson@virgin.net

Crediton - Near railway station.
Mrs. S. Pugsley, Great Park Farm, Crediton. EX17 3PR
Tel. 01363 772050
www.creditonbandb.co.uk
email: susan.pugsley@btconnect.com

Bridgwater - In village, 2 miles off Cannon Roundabout.
Apple View & Bramley Lodge, Temple Farm, Chedzoy,
Bridgwater. TA7 8QR
Tel. 01278 423201
www.apple-view.co.uk
email: temple_farm@hotmail.com

Chepstow
Jane Cooper, 1st Hurdle Guest House, 9-10 Upper Church Street,
Chepstow, Monmouthshire. NP16 5EX
Tel. 01291 622189
www.firsthurdle.com

Hereford - 300yds from Cathedral.
Holly Tree Guest House, 21 Barton Road, Hereford. HR4 0AY
Tel. 01432 357845
www.hollytreehereford.co.uk
email: elaine@hollytreehereford.co.uk

Ludlow
Mr. Ray Foster, The Mount, 61 Gravel Hill, Ludlow,
Shropshire. SY8 1QS
Tel. 01584 874084
www.themountludlow.co.uk
email: rooms@themountludlow.co.uk

Whitchurch - Just off town centre.
Mrs. D. Clubbe, Pheasant Walk, Terrick Road, Whitchurch,
Shrop. SY13 4JZ
Tel. 01948 667118

Warrington
Laburnham Guest House, 106-112 Wilderspool Causeway,
Warrington, Cheshire. WA4 6PU
Tel. 01925 575569
www.warringtonguesthouses.com
email: Joanne@jwilson6.wanadoo.co.uk

Wigan - Town centre.
Maple Hotel, 35 Upper Dicconson Road, Wigan,
Greater Manchester. WN1 2AG
Tel. 01942 243537
www.maplehotel.co.uk
Secure lock up.

Bilsborrow - North of Preston on A6
Mrs Jayne Bolton, Olde Duncombe House, Garstang Road,
Bilsborrow, Preston. PR3 0RE
Tel. 01995 640336
email: oldedunc@aol.com

Kendal - On route
Mrs Jayne Bolton, Glenholme Guest House, 43 Milnthorpe Rd,
Kendal. LA9 5QG
Tel. 01539 721489
www.glenholmekendal.co.uk
email: glynis@glenholme43.freeserve.co.uk
or info@.glenholmekendal.co.uk

Shap - On route
Fell House, Main St, Shap, Cumbria. CA10 3NY
Tel. 01931 716343
www.fellhouse.com
email: louis_mushandu@talk21.com

Carlisle - Near bus and railway station in centre.
Cornerways Guest House, 107 Warwick Rd, Carlisle. CA1 1EA
Tel. 01228 521733
www.cornerwaysbandb.co.uk
email: info@cornerwaysbandb.co.uk

Lockerbie
Tarras Guesthouse, 29-31 Mains Street, Lockerbie. DG11 2DG
Tel. 01576 203849
email: reception@tarrasbandb.co.uk

Crawford - On route
Holmelands Country House, 22 Carlisle Road, Crawford. ML12 6TW
Tel. 01864 502753
www.holmlandscountryhouse.co.uk
email: cerena_soances@btconnect.com

Airdrie – 2 miles north of Airdrie on A73.
Fairview B&B, Stirling Road Stand, Airdrie, ML6 7FP
Tel. 01236 830234
www.fairviewbedandbreakfast.co.uk
email: robert830234@aol.com

Stirling
Mrs J Dougall, 14 Melville Terrace, Stirling. FK8 2NE
Tel. 01786 814603
www.dougallguesthouse.co.uk
email: mjdougall@hotmail.com

Crieff – In centre of town off the A85
Galvelmore House, 5 Galvelmore Street, Crieff, Perthshire. PH7 4BY
Tel. 01764 655721
www.galvelmore.co.uk
email: katy@galvelmore.co.uk

Aberfeldy
Coshieville House, Coshieville, By Aberfeldy, Perthshire. PH15 2NE
Tel. 01887 830319
www.aberfeldybandb.com
email: coshieville@btinternet.com

Kingussie
Dunmhor Guest House, 67 High Street, Kingussie.
Tel. 01540 662269
www.dunmhor-guesthouse.net
email: audrey.downey@ukgateway.net

Inverness
Dunhallin House, 164 Culduthel Road, Inverness,
Inverness-shire. IV2 4BH
Tel. 01463 220824
www.dunhallin.co.uk
email: info@dunhallin.co.uk

Culbokie – Black Isle – 700yds from A9
Netherton, Culbokie, Dingwall, Ross-shire. IV7 8JH
Tel. 01349 87666
www.nethertonfarm.co.uk
email: rooms@nethertonfarm.co.uk
B&B + bunkhouse & camping by arrangement.

Golspie
Culmarron B&B, 1 Bhraggie Drive, Golspie, Sutherland. KW10 6SX
Tel. 01408 633434

John O'Groats
Sea View Hotel, John O'Groats, Caithness. KW1 4YR
Tel 01955 611220
www.seaviewjohnogroats.co.uk
email: seaviewhotel@btinternet.com

Photo 12. The Last House in Scotland.
Register Your Finish Here or in the Groats Inn (Background)

Main Towns/Villages on Route

Lands End

Penzance

Hayle (just off)

Redruth (just off)

Bodmin (just off)

Launceston (just off)

Okehampton

Crediton

Tiverton

Taunton

Bridgwater

Bristol

Chepstow

Monmouth

Hereford

Leominster (just off)

Ludlow

Shrewsbury

Whitchurch

Warrington

Wigan

Preston

Lancaster

Kendal

Penrith

Carlisle

Gretna

Lockerbie (just off)

Lanark

Airdrie

Cumbernauld

Denny

Stirling

Dunblane

Crieff

Aberfeldy

Kingussie (just off)

Aviemore (just off)

Inverness (just off)

Golspie

Brora

Helmsdale

Wick

John O'Groats

CTC (Cyclists Touring Club)

Parklands,
Railton Road,
Guildford
Surrey
GU2 9JX
0844 736 8450
cycling@ctc.org.uk
www.ctc.org.uk

This is Britain's largest cycling association with around 70,000 members. CTC exists to promote cycling as a means of transport and travel, and campaigns to protect cyclists' interests. A bi-monthly magazine and weekly e-newsletter keep members in touch. A number of large national events and rallies are organised and 250 local groups plan and lead rides all over the country.

By becoming a member of CTC, you have access to advice and a whole package of information and services, as well as leaflets covering many aspects of cycling, from buying a bike to riding for charity and transporting bikes on trains and buses. There is also a library of over 800 routes Worldwide to use or get ideas from.

CTC is a well organised professional club and I recommend joining.

Useful Addresses & Websites

Lands End - John O'Groats End to End Club
Lands End & John O'Groats Club
Lands End
Sennen
Cornwall
TR19 7AA
Tel. 01736 871501 ex 322
email: lejogclub.landsend@tiscali.co.uk
www.endtoenders.co.uk

Advice and information, magazines and special offers for club members.

The Land's End to John O'Groats Association
Find out more about this club at
www.landsend-johnogroats-assoc.com

This is open to anyone who has completed the journey from end to end by any means.

National Rail Services.
Tel. 08457 484950
www.nationalrail.co.uk

Scotrail Ticket Purchases.
Tel. 08457 550033

Stagecoach Buses
Tel. 01463 710555
www.stagecoach.com

Buses from Inverness to John O'Groats

Independent Hostel Guide
Tel. 01629 580427
www.independenthostelguide.co.uk

Youth Hostels Association

Trevelyan House,
Dimple Road,
Matlock,
Derbyshire,
DE4 3YH
Tel. 0870 770 8868
www.yha.org.uk
Reservations – 0870 770 6113
Email – reservations@yha.org.uk

Scottish Youth Hostels Association

7, Glebe Crescent,
Stirling,
FK8 2JA
Tel. 01786 891400
www.syha.org.uk
Reservations – 0870 155 3255
Email – reservations@syha.org.uk

Many hostels are closed during the day, phones may be switched to central reservations.
All hostels offer a free 'book a bed ahead' service.
Hostels may be self catering only, please check.
In summer months especially, book well in advance if you can.

The route described in this book was the one used by the author for cycling both ways; it was checked in late 2008 and believed to be correct at the time of publication.

Hopefully you have enjoyed this memorable expedition and gained as much pleasure from cycling the route as he did. Please visit Challenge Publications website at: -

www.chall-pub.co.uk

A wide selection of guides covering the UK are available including Millennium Cycle Rides in 1066 Country, covering cycling routes in and around East Sussex and containing everything you need to know on a set of laminated cards.

A special cyclist's end-to-end logbook is available where you can record each day's epic journey. Email challenge publications for a free pricelist.

On our website you will find some interesting and different walks around the British Isles, which are picturesque and enjoyable including The National 3 Peaks Walk and John O'Groats to Lands End walking guides.

Should you wish to comment on this book, send for a free pricelist or give further information to help keep the book updated then please write to the address below or email Brian at: - challengepublications@yahoo.co.uk.
An acknowledgement will be given: -

Challenge Publications
7, Earlsmere Drive,
Ardsley,
Barnsley.
S71 5HH

Expedition Daily Diary

Use the following points when recording your experiences, highs and lows of your epic journey.

DAY ONE

Start Time: . . . . Finish Time: . . . .

Weather: . . . .

. . . .

Distance Travelled: . . . .

From: . . . .

To: . . . .

Overnight Stay: . . . .

. . . .

Special Points: . . . .

. . . .

. . . .

. . . .

. . . .

. . . .

. . . .

. . . .

. . . .

. . . .

DAY TWO

Start Time: . . . . Finish Time: . . . .

Weather: . . . .

. . . .

Distance Travelled: . . . .

From: . . . .

To: . . . .

Overnight Stay: . . . .

. . . .

Special Points: . . . .

. . . .

. . . .

. . . .

. . . .

. . . .

. . . .

. . . .

. . . .

. . . .

. . . .

. . . .

. . . .

. . . .

. . . .

DAY THREE

Start Time: . . . . Finish Time: . . . .

Weather: . . . .

. . . .

Distance Travelled: . . . .

From: . . . .

To: . . . .

Overnight Stay: . . . .

. . . .

Special Points: . . . .

. . . .

. . . .

. . . .

. . . .

. . . .

. . . .

. . . .

. . . .

. . . .

. . . .

. . . .

. . . .

DAY FOUR

Start Time: . . . . Finish Time: . . . .

Weather: . . . .

. . . .

Distance Travelled: . . . .

From: . . . .

To: . . . .

Overnight Stay: . . . .

. . . .

Special Points: . . . .

. . . .

. . . .

. . . .

. . . .

. . . .

. . . .

. . . .

. . . .

. . . .

. . . .

. . . .

. . . .

. . . .

DAY FIVE

Start Time: . . . . Finish Time: . . . .

Weather: . . . .

. . . .

Distance Travelled: . . . .

From: . . . .

To: . . . .

Overnight Stay: . . . .

. . . .

Special Points: . . . .

. . . .

. . . .

. . . .

. . . .

. . . .

. . . .

. . . .

. . . .

. . . .

. . . .

. . . .

. . . .

. . . .

DAY SIX

Start Time: . . . . Finish Time: . . . .

Weather: . . . .

. . . .

Distance Travelled: . . . .

From: . . . .

To: . . . .

Overnight Stay: . . . .

. . . .

Special Points: . . . .

. . . .

. . . .

. . . .

. . . .

. . . .

. . . .

. . . .

. . . .

. . . .

. . . .

. . . .

. . . .

. . . .

DAY SEVEN

Start Time: . . . . Finish Time: . . . .

Weather: . . . .

. . . .

Distance Travelled: . . . .

From: . . . .

To: . . . .

Overnight Stay: . . . .

. . . .

Special Points: . . . .

. . . .

. . . .

. . . .

. . . .

. . . .

. . . .

. . . .

. . . .

. . . .

. . . .

. . . .

. . . .

. . . .

DAY EIGHT

Start Time: . . . . Finish Time: . . . .

Weather: . . . .

. . . .

Distance Travelled: . . . .

From: . . . .

To: . . . .

Overnight Stay: . . . .

. . . .

Special Points: . . . .

. . . .

. . . .

. . . .

. . . .

. . . .

. . . .

. . . .

. . . .

. . . .

. . . .

. . . .

. . . .

. . . .

DAY NINE

Start Time: . . . . Finish Time: . . . .

Weather: . . . .

. . . .

Distance Travelled: . . . .

From: . . . .

To: . . . .

Overnight Stay: . . . .

. . . .

Special Points: . . . .

. . . .

. . . .

. . . .

. . . .

. . . .

. . . .

. . . .

. . . .

. . . .

. . . .

. . . .

. . . .

. . . .

DAY TEN

Start Time: . . . . Finish Time: . . . .

Weather: . . . .

. . . .

Distance Travelled: . . . .

From: . . . .

To: . . . .

Overnight Stay: . . . .

. . . .

Special Points: . . . .

. . . .

. . . .

. . . .

. . . .

. . . .

. . . .

. . . .

. . . .

. . . .

. . . .

. . . .

. . . .